Make Origami
INSECTS and SPIDERS

by Ruth Owen

PowerKiDS
press™

New York

Published in 2018 by **The Rosen Publishing Group, Inc.**
29 East 21st Street, New York, NY 10010

CATALOGING-IN-PUBLICATION DATA

Names: Owen, Ruth.
Title: Make origami insects and spiders / Ruth Owen.
Description: New York : PowerKids Press, 2018. | Series: Animal kingdom origami |
  Includes index.
Identifiers: ISBN 9781499433548 (pbk.) | ISBN 9781499433487 (library bound) |
  ISBN 9781499433364 (6 pack)
Subjects: LCSH: Origami--Juvenile literature. | Insects in art--Juvenile literature.
Classification: LCC TT872.5 O94 2018 | DDC 736'.982--dc23

First Edition

Produced for Rosen by Ruth Owen Books

Designer: Emma Randall
Photo Credits: Courtesy of Ruth Owen Books and Shutterstock.

Manufactured in the United States of America
CPSIA Compliance Information: Batch BS17PK: For Further Information contact Rosen Publishing, New York, New York at 1-800-237-9932.

Contents

What Is an Insect? 4

What Is a Spider? 5

Ladybugs:
Flying Beetles 6

Grasshoppers:
Super Jumpers 10

Butterflies:
Smelling for Food 14

Caterpillars:
A Butterfly's Life Cycle 18

Spiders:
Eight-Legged Hunters 22

Spiderwebs:
Hunting with Silk 26

Glossary 30

Websites 31

Index 32

What Is an Insect?

Insects are small animals with six legs and a pair of **antennae**. Scientists have studied and identified about 1 million different **species** of insects—so far. They believe there may actually be about 6 million different types on Earth!

Insects are **invertebrates**, which means they do not have a backbone. Instead of a skeleton, insects have a hard shell called an **exoskeleton**.

Insects use their antennae for smelling, tasting, and gathering information about their environment.

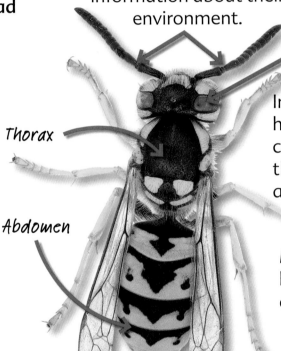

Head

Thorax

Abdomen

Insects' bodies have three parts called the head, thorax, and abdomen.

Most insects have two pairs of wings.

Stink Bug Life Cycle: Egg ➞ Nymph ➞ Adult

Some insects, such as grasshoppers and stink bugs, go through three life stages. Others, such as butterflies and moths, have four life stages.

Eggs

Stink bug nymphs

Adult stink bug

What Is a Spider?

A spider is an invertebrate with a tough exoskeleton, eight legs, and a body in two parts, called the cephalothorax and abdomen.

A spider has three life stages:

Egg ➡ Spiderling ➡ Adult

A female spider lays her eggs and wraps them in an egg sac made of silk.

Egg sac

Tiny spiderlings hatch from the eggs.

Spiders have two short, leg-like parts called pedipalps. They use their pedipalps for gathering information. Some spiders use them to capture prey.

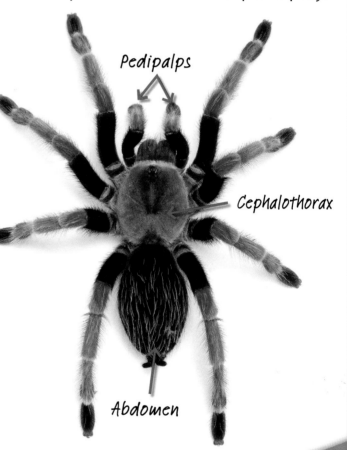

Pedipalps

Cephalothorax

Abdomen

There are about 35,000 different species of spiders.

Let's get folding and learn more about insects and spiders!

Ladybugs: Flying Beetles

One of the most easily recognizable insects is the ladybug. Ladybugs are a type of beetle. Most ladybugs feed on tiny aphids and other insects. A ladybug might eat 5,000 aphids during its year-long lifetime.

While we often see ladybugs walking about on plants, these little beetles can actually fly. A ladybug has a pair of spotted, thick, shell-like wing covers called elytra. These protective covers open to reveal the long, thin flight wings underneath. A ladybug beats its wings to take off. Then, as it flies, its elytra stay open, but they don't actually help the ladybug fly.

Elytra

Ladybug

Wings

FOLD A LADYBUG

You will need:
• One square piece of red paper
• A black marker

Step 1:
Fold the paper in half diagonally, and crease.

Step 2:
Fold the paper in half again, crease, and unfold.

Step 3:
Fold the right-hand side of the model into the center crease, and crease hard.

Repeat on the left-hand side.

Step 4:
Now to make the ladybug's elytra, or wing covers, fold the right-hand point back down, and crease.

Fold each elytron at a slight angle, so the ladybug's body can be seen underneath.

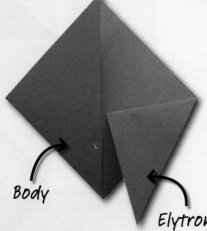

Body

Elytron

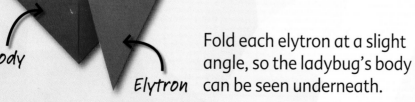

Fold down the top point of the model along the dotted line, crease hard, and then unfold.

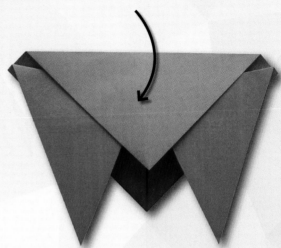

Step 6:

Now fold down the top point to the crease you've just made. Then fold down the top of the model again along the dotted line, and crease.

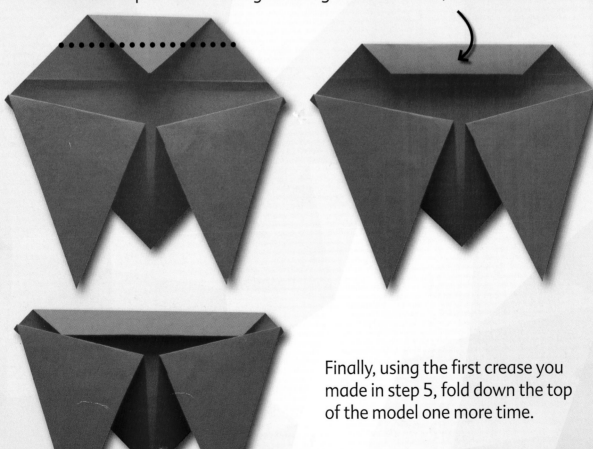

Finally, using the first crease you made in step 5, fold down the top of the model one more time.

This area should be narrow to create the ladybug's head.

Step 7:

Turn the model over and fold in the two sides so that they meet at the center crease.

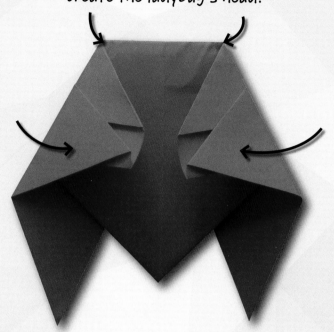

Head

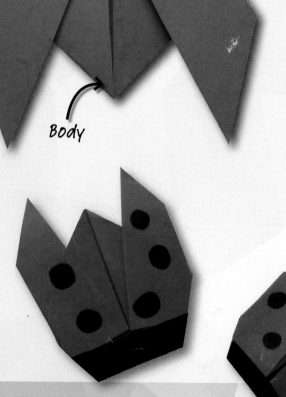

Body

Step 8:

Turn the model over, color the head black, and add some spots. Your ladybug is complete!

Grasshoppers: Super Jumpers

Grasshoppers are insects with a pair of large back legs that allow them to leap long distances. A grasshopper's folded back legs allow it to push off from the ground with lots of force and speed. It has claws on its feet to keep them from skidding as it pushes off.

Grasshoppers jump to escape from **predators**, to take off when flying, and to move from place to place. In a single jump, a grasshopper can cover a distance of about 3 feet (1 m)!

FOLD A GRASSHOPPER

You will need:
- A square piece of paper in your choice of color
- A black marker

Step 1:

Fold the paper in half diagonally, and crease hard.

Fold in half again, and crease.

Step 2:

Turn the triangle you've just made so that the longest side is at the bottom. Working with the top layer of paper only, fold the left-hand point over to meet the right-hand point, crease hard.

Open up here

Pocket

Square

Now open up the pocket you've just made. Gently squash the pocket down to make a square.

Step 3:

Turn the model over. Now open up the triangle on the right-hand side to create a pocket, and squash down as you did in step 2.

Turn the square you've now made so the open edges are at the bottom.

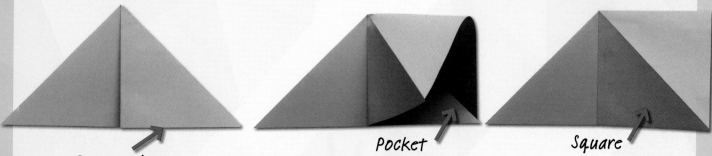

Open up here

Open edge

11

Step 4:

Working with just the top layer of paper, fold in the two side points to the center, and crease hard.

Now fold down the top point, and crease hard.

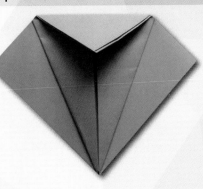

Step 5:

Next, unfold the three folds you've just made to create a beak-like pocket.

Beak-like pocket

Fold and squash down the sides of the beak-like pocket to make a diamond shape.

Step 6:

Turn the model over and repeat what you did in step 4: folding in the two side points and folding down the center point.

Next, open out the three folds you've just made to create a beak-like pocket.

Fold and squash the pocket to create a diamond shape.

Step 7:

Working with just the top layer of paper, fold the two side points into the center, and crease hard.

Turn the model over and repeat on the other side.

Step 8:

Now, fold down point A, as shown, and crease.

Next, fold point B behind the model, as shown, and crease.

Center crease

Head

Wings

Legs

Step 9:

Turn the model 90 degrees counterclockwise. Now fold the model in half along the center crease.

Take hold of the wings section and gently pull upward away from the legs.

Step 10:

Take hold of the top leg and fold it upward.

Then, about halfway along the leg, fold it back down to create the grasshopper's knee.

Step 11:

Repeat step 10 on the other leg.

Finally, give your origami grasshopper a face.

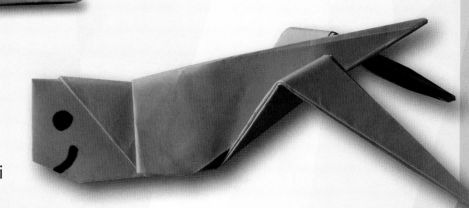

Butterflies: Smelling for Food

Butterfly experts, called lepidopterists, think there are more than 20,000 different species of butterflies. Most butterflies feed on nectar. They drink it from flowers through a long, straw-like mouthpart called a proboscis. Butterflies have special **cells** on their antennae that help them smell for food and for **mates**. Butterflies can also detect food using cells on their feet and legs.

Female butterflies lay their eggs on plants that will become food for their caterpillars once they hatch. A female butterfly may smell a plant with her feet to make sure it's the right type of plant for her caterpillars to eat.

Antennae

A curled-up proboscis

Six legs

FOLD A BUTTERFLY

You will need:
• A square piece of paper in your choice of color or pattern

Step 1:

Fold the paper in half diagonally, crease, and unfold. Then fold the paper in half in the opposite direction, crease, and unfold.

Step 2:

Now fold the four points into the center of the model, and crease well.

Step 3:

Turn the model over. Now fold all four points into the center, and crease hard.

Step 4:

Now unfold all the folds you've just made. Your piece of paper should look like this.

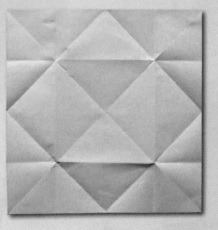

Step 5:

Now fold in the two sides of the paper so that they meet in the center, and crease.

Step 6:

Unfold and open out the top half of the model. Then using the creases you made in the earlier stages, gently squash and flatten the top of the model.

Step 7:

Repeat step 6 on the bottom half of the model.

Step 8:

Now fold the model in half so that the open sections are at the top.

Step 9:

Now take hold of the model's top left-hand point, fold it down along the dotted line, and crease. Repeat on the top right-hand point. You should only be folding down the top layer of paper.

Step 10:

Now make a small fold along the dotted lines on each side of the model. Crease well.

Step 11:

Now fold the model in half along its center.

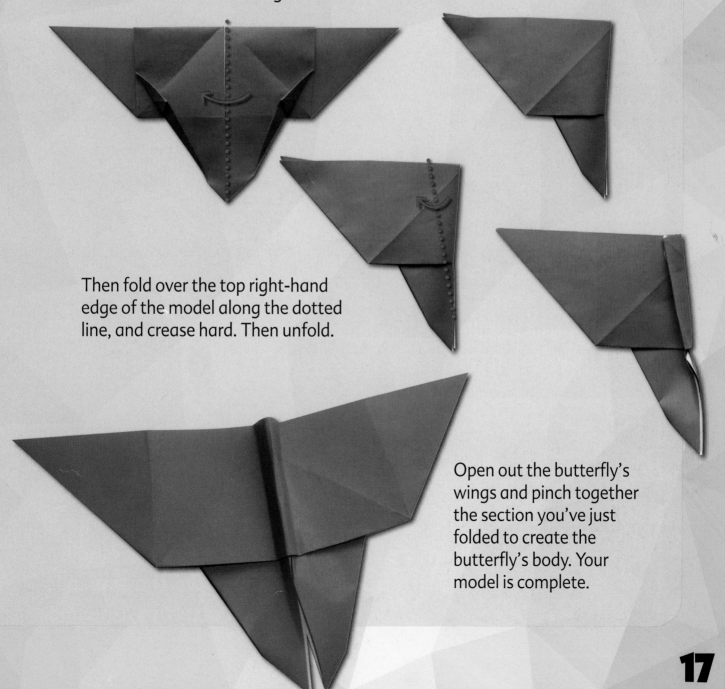

Then fold over the top right-hand edge of the model along the dotted line, and crease hard. Then unfold.

Open out the butterfly's wings and pinch together the section you've just folded to create the butterfly's body. Your model is complete.

Caterpillars: A Butterfly's Life Cycle

A butterfly has four different life cycle stages. The changes it goes through are known as **metamorphosis**.

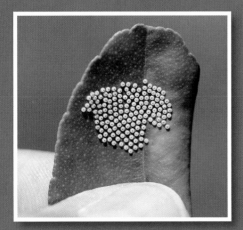

Butterfly eggs

A butterfly begins its life as an egg. A caterpillar, or larva, hatches from the egg and immediately starts munching on plants. Like all insects, a caterpillar has six legs. It also has body parts known as false legs for holding onto plants.

False legs

6 true legs

Chrysalis case

Chrysalis

A butterfly forming inside a chrysalis

A butterfly emerging

A caterpillar grows and grows, and then becomes a **chrysalis** inside a case, or skin. During this life cycle stage the insect's body changes shape. Finally it emerges from the chrysalis case as a butterfly with wings.

FOLD A CATERPILLAR

You will need:
- A square piece of paper in your choice of color
- A black marker

Step 1:

Fold the paper in half diagonally, and crease.

Step 2:

Fold up the long side of the triangle, and crease hard.

Step 3:

Open out and flatten the paper. Now fold in the top and bottom points along the creases you made in step 2.

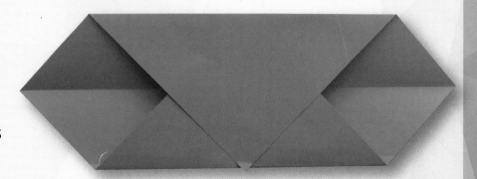

Step 4:

Turn the model 90 degrees clockwise. Now fold up the bottom point of the model, and crease.

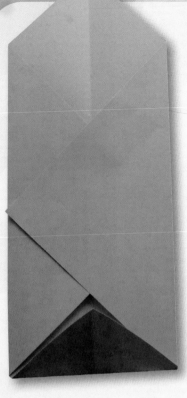

Then fold the point back down, creating a small pleat, and crease.

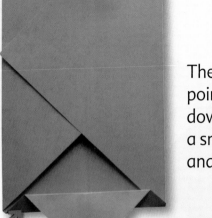

Pleat

Step 5:

Next, you will make four pleated folds (along the dotted lines) to create the sections of the caterpillar's body.

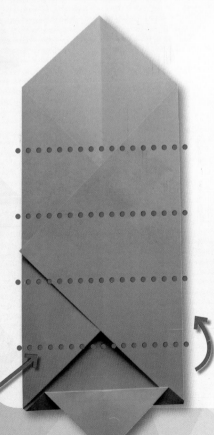

Fold up here

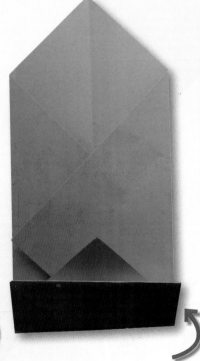

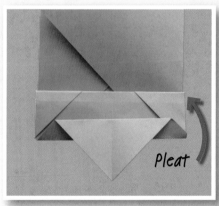

Pleat

Begin by folding up the bottom of the body. Crease hard and then fold back down to make a small pleat.

Step 6:

Fold up and then pleat along the next dotted line.

Top of model

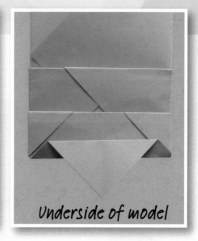

Underside of model

Repeat until you've made the four pleated folds of the caterpillar's body.

Top of caterpillar's body

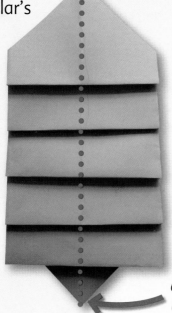

Folded head point

Center crease

Step 7:

Fold the model in half along the center crease. Crease hard.

You can use a paperclip to hold the two sides together for the next stage.

Fold down the head point of the model, crease hard, and unfold.

Step 8:

Now open out the model. Draw on two eyes and then tuck in the point of the head along the folds you made in step 7.

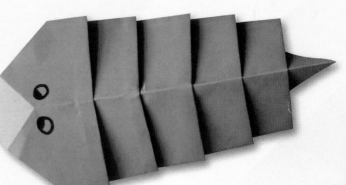

Your origami caterpillar is complete!

Spiders: Eight-Legged Hunters

All spiders are **carnivores** that hunt and feed on other animals. Most spiders feed on insects. A spider's digestive process begins before it's even swallowed a mouthful. Once a spider has caught an insect, it vomits digestive juices over its meal or into its **prey's** exoskeleton. The juices break down the animal's soft body parts, turning them into a soupy liquid. Then the spider sucks its meal of bug soup into its mouth.

Tarantulas are large spiders that kill with their bite. A tarantula injects **venom** into its prey with its **fangs**. Tarantulas may feed on animals such as mice, small birds, and frogs.

A tarantula

FOLD A SPIDER

You will need:
• A square piece of paper in your choice of color
• Scissors

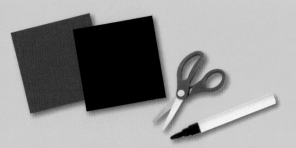

Step 1:

Fold the paper in half along the dotted lines, crease, and then unfold.

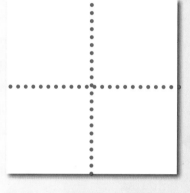

Turn the paper over. Fold in half along the dotted lines, crease, and unfold.

Step 2:

Place the paper white side down. When viewed from above, it should now look like this.

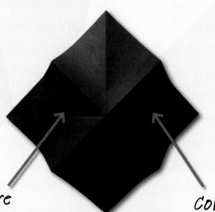

Collapse in here

Pick up the paper, and using the creases you've just made, collapse in the sides of the model, as shown here.

Collapse in here

Squash down

Step 3:

Squash down on the model to form a square.

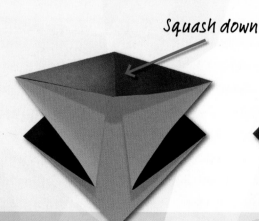

Step 4:

Take hold of the right-hand side point of the square (just the top layer of paper). Lift it up, open it out slightly, and then gently squash it flat to form an upside-down kite shape.

Right-hand point of model, lifted and opened out

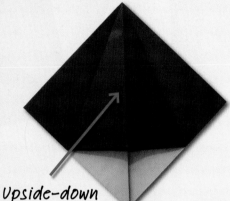

Upside-down kite shape

Now, opening and closing each of the other three sides of your model in turns, repeat what you've just done on the other three points until your model looks like this.

Step 5:

Next, working with just one diamond and the top layer of paper, fold each of the bottom edges into the center of the model, crease hard, and unfold.

A

Now gently lift up the section marked A to form a pocket. Then, using the creases you've just made, squash and flatten the pocket to create a small kite shape.

Small kite shape

Pocket

Again, move around your model, repeating everything you've done in step 5 three more times until your model looks like this.

Step 6:

Now open up your model at a flat section that contains no kite shape. Working with just the top layer of paper, fold the two sides into the center crease along the dotted lines, and crease hard. Now repeat on the model's other three flat sections.

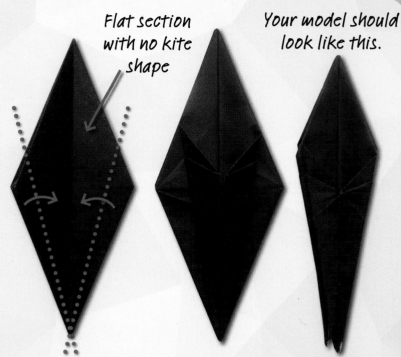

Flat section with no kite shape

Your model should look like this.

Cut up the center of each long point.

Step 7:

Your model will now have four long, pointed sections. Carefully cut up the center of each point to create eight points, or legs.

Open up the model to a section that contains a small kite shape, and begin folding the legs out to the side.

Two points (or legs) created by cutting

To round off the tarantula's body, you can fold the end point under.

Open out a section with a kite shape.

Fold the point of the body under here.

Step 8:

Fold some of the legs forward and some backward to create a realistic shape for your origami tarantula.

Spiderwebs: Hunting with Silk

Some species of spiders build webs made of silk for capturing prey. The silk threads come from organs called spinnerets beneath the spider's abdomen. As a spider creates its web, the silk squeezes from its spinnerets like toothpaste from a tube. At first the silk is liquid, but it quickly hardens. Some of the web's threads are made of sticky silk.

Once its silk trap is complete, the spider usually waits on the web or nearby. When an insect comes into contact with the web's sticky threads, it becomes trapped. Then the spider rushes to its prey and imprisons it in silk—ready for eating!

FOLD A SPIDERWEB

You will need:

- A sheet of white printer paper
- A ruler
- A pencil
- Scissors

Step 1:

Fold the paper in half, and crease.

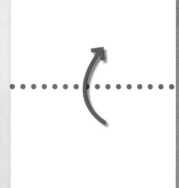

Step 2:

Now fold in half again, but don't fully crease. Just make a small "pinch crease" to mark the center point. Then unfold.

Pinch crease at center point.

Step 3:

Next, fold and roll the sides of the paper into a cone shape. The base of the cone should be the center point you marked with the pinch crease. Carefully flatten the cone so the edges line up.

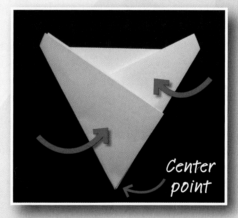

Center point

Your model should look like this.

Step 4:

Now cut along the dotted line to leave a triangle.

Cut along the dotted line.

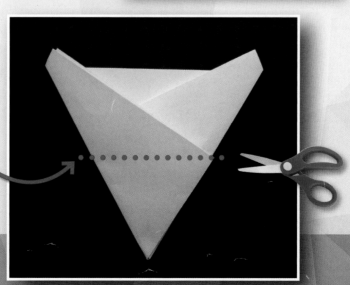

Step 5:

Next, draw eight horizontal lines across the triangle to divide it into nine sections. It doesn't matter if the sections aren't exactly equal, as this will add to the web's pattern.

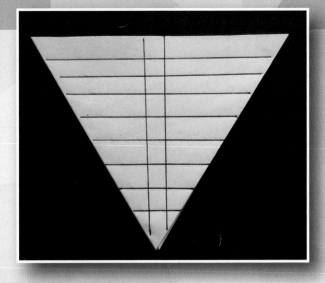

Also draw two vertical lines.

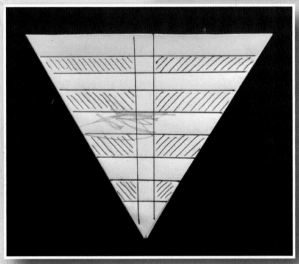

Step 6:

Now shade in alternate horizontal sections, as shown.

Step 7:

Next, carefully cut out all the areas that you shaded in.

Make sure you don't cut through the center spine of the model.

Step 8:

Finally, open out the model and your spiderweb is complete!

The paper spiderweb is made using kirigami. This is an art form that uses paper folding and cutting to make models.

Glossary

antennae
Long, thin body parts on the heads of insects. Each antenna is used by the insect to gather information about its environment.

carnivores
Animals that eat only meat.

cells
Very tiny parts of a living thing. Most cells can only be seen through a microscope.

chrysalis
The stage in a butterfly or moth's life when it develops into an adult.

exoskeleton
A hard, protective outer covering on the body of an animal such as an insect or spider.

fangs
Long, sharp teeth that animals such as snakes and spiders use to inject venom into prey.

invertebrates
Animals without a backbone. Many animals belong to this group, including insects, spiders, crabs and lobsters, snails, worms, octopuses, and jellyfish.

mates
Partners of the opposite sex with which animals produce young.

metamorphosis
The process of transforming from one thing to another. A caterpillar goes through a metamorphosis to become a butterfly.

predators
Animals that hunt and kill other animals for food.

prey
An animal that is hunted by another animal as food.

venom
Poison that is injected into a person or animal through a bite or sting.

species
One type of living thing. The members of a species look alike and can produce young together.

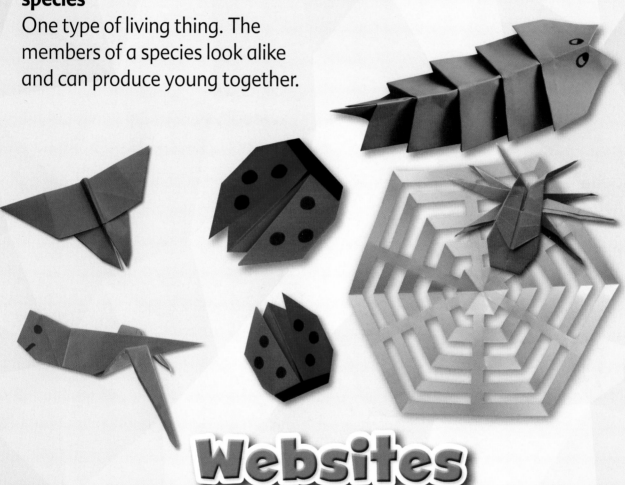

Websites

Due to the changing nature of internet links, PowerKids Press has developed an online list of websites related to the subject of this book. This site is updated regularly. Please use this link to access the list:

www.powerkidslinks.com/ako/insects

Index

A
antennae, 4, 14

B
butterflies, 4, 14–15, 16–17, 18

C
caterpillars, 14, 18–19, 20–21

E
eggs, 4–5, 14, 18
exoskeletons, 4–5, 22

F
fangs, 22
flying, 6, 10
food and feeding, 5, 6, 14, 18, 22

G
grasshoppers, 4, 10–11, 12–13

H
hunting, 5, 22, 26

I
insects, 4, 6–7, 8–9, 10–11,
     12–13, 14–15, 16–17, 18–19,
     20–21, 22, 26
invertebrates, 4–5

L
ladybugs, 6–7, 8–9
legs, 4–5, 10, 14, 18
life cycles, 4–5, 18

S
silk, 5, 26
spiderlings, 5
spiders, 22–23, 24–25, 26–27,
     28–29
spiderwebs, 26–27, 28–29
stink bugs, 4

T
tarantulas, 22

V
venom, 22

W
wings, 4, 6, 18